WOOD PELLET

GRILL AND SMOKER

COOKBOOK

PIT BOSS POULTRY RECIPES

**Easy and Delicious Recipes
to smoke and Grill and Enjoy
with your Family and Friends**

Steve Harris

Copyright © 2021 by Steve Harris

Legal Disclaimer

The information contained in this book and its contents is not designed to replace any form of medical or professional advice; and is not meant to replace the need for independent medical, financial, legal, or other professional advice or service that may require. The content and information in this book have been provided for educational and entertainment purposes only.

The content and information contained in this book have been compiled from sources deemed reliable, and they are accurate to the best of the Author's knowledge, information and belief.

However, the Author cannot guarantee its accuracy and validity and therefore cannot be held liable for any errors and/or omissions.

Further, changes are periodically made to this book as needed. Where appropriate and/or necessary, you must consult a professional (including but not limited to your doctor, attorney, financial advisor, or other such professional) before using any of the suggested remedies, techniques, and/or information in this book.

Upon using this book's contents and information, you agree to hold harmless the Author from any damaged, costs and expenses, including any legal fees potentially resulting from the application of any of the information in this book. This disclaimer applies to any loss, damages, or injury caused by the use and application of this book's content, whether directly and indirectly, whether for breach of contract, tort, negligence, personal injury, criminal intent, or under any other circumstances.

You agree to accept all risks of using the information presented in this book. You agree that by continuing to read this book, where appropriate and/or necessary, you shall consult a professional (including but not limited to your doctor, attorney, financial advisor, or other such professional) before remedies, techniques, and/or information in **this book.**

TABLE OF CONTENTS

PIT BOSS Poultry Recipes

Pit boss Chile Lime Chicken

Prep Time: 2 Minutes; Cook Time: 15 Minutes

Servings: 1

INGREDIENTS:

- ➢ 1 chicken breast
- ➢ 1 tbsp. oil
- ➢ 1 tbsp. spice ology Chile Lime Seasoning

DIRECTIONS:

1. Preheat your Pit boss to 4000F.
2. Brush the chicken breast with oil then sprinkle the chile-lime seasoning and salt.
3. Place the chicken breast on the grill and cook for 7 minutes on each side or until the internal temperature reaches 1650F.
4. Serve when hot and enjoy.

Nutrition: Calories 131, Total fat 5g, Saturated fat 1g, Total carbs 4g, Net carbs 3g Protein 19g, Sugars 1g, Fiber 1g, Sodium 235mg

Pit boss Grilled Buffalo Chicken

Prep Time: 5 Minutes; Cook Time: 10 Minutes

Servings: 6

INGREDIENTS:

➢ 5 chicken breasts, boneless and skinless

➢ 2 tbsp. homemade BBQ rub

➢ 1 cup homemade Cholula Buffalo sauce

DIRECTIONS:

1. Preheat the Pit boss to 4000F.

2. Slice the chicken breast lengthwise into strips. Season the slices with BBQ rub.

3. Place the chicken slices on the grill and paint both sides with buffalo sauce.

4. Cook for 4 minutes with the lid closed. Flip the breasts, paint again with sauce, and cook until the internal temperature reaches 1650F.

5. Remove the chicken from the Pit boss and serve when warm.

Nutrition: Calories 176, Total fat 4g, Saturated fat 1g, Total carbs 1g, Net carbs 1g Protein 32g, Sugars 1g, Fiber 0g, Sodium 631mg

Pit boss Sheet Pan Chicken Fajitas

Prep Time: 10 Minutes; Cook Time: 10 Minutes

Servings: 10

INGREDIENTS:

- ➢ 2 lb. chicken breast
- ➢ 1 onion, sliced.
- ➢ 1 red bell pepper seeded and sliced.
- ➢ 1 orange-red bell pepper seeded and sliced.
- ➢ 1 tbsp. salt
- ➢ 1/2 tbsp. onion powder
- ➢ 1/2 tbsp. granulated garlic
- ➢ 2 tbsp. Spice ologist Chile Margarita Seasoning
- ➢ 2 tbsp. oil

DIRECTIONS:

1. Preheat the Pit boss to 4500F and line a baking sheet with parchment paper.
2. In a mixing bowl, combine seasonings and oil then toss with the peppers and chicken.
3. Place the baking sheet in the Pit boss and let heat for 10 minutes with the lid closed.
4. Open the lid and place the veggies and the chicken in a single layer. Close the lid and cook for 10 minutes or until the chicken is no longer pink.

5. Serve with warm tortillas and top with your favorite toppings.

Nutrition: Calories 211, Total fat 6g, Saturated fat 1g, Total carbs 5g, Net carbs 4g Protein 29g, Sugars 4g, Fiber 1g, Sodium 360mg

Pit boss Asian Miso Chicken wings

Prep Time: 15 Minutes; Cook Time: 25 Minutes

Servings: 6

INGREDIENTS:

- ➤ 2 lb. chicken wings
- ➤ 3/4 cup soy
- ➤ 1/2 cup pineapple juice
- ➤ 1 tbsp. sriracha
- ➤ 1/8 cup miso
- ➤ 1/8 cup gochujang
- ➤ 1/2 cup water
- ➤ 1/2 cup oil
- ➤ Togarashi

DIRECTIONS:

1. Preheat the Pit boss to 3750F
2. Combine all the ingredients except togarashi in a zip lock bag. Toss until the chicken wings are well coated. Refrigerate for 12 hours.
3. Pace the wings on the grill grates and close the lid. Cook for 25 minutes or until the internal temperature reaches 1650F.
4. Remove the wings from the Pit boss and sprinkle Togarashi.
5. Serve when hot and enjoy.

Nutrition: Calories 703, Total fat 56g, Saturated fat 14g, Total carbs 24g, Net carbs 23g Protein 27g, Sugars 6g, Fiber 1g, Sodium 1156mg

Yan's Grilled Quarters

Prep Time: 20 minutes (additional 2-4 hours marinade); Cook Time: 1 to 1.5 hours

Servings: 4

INGREDIENTS:

- ➤ 4 fresh or thawed frozen chicken quarters
- ➤ 4-6 glasses of extra virgin olive oil
- ➤ 4 tablespoons of Yang's original dry lab

DIRECTIONS:

1. Configure a wood pellet smoker grill for indirect cooking and use the pellets to preheat to 325 ° F.
2. Place chicken on grill and cook at 325 ° F for 1 hour.
3. After one hour, raise the pit temperature to 400 ° F to finish the chicken and crisp the skin.
4. When the inside temperature of the thickest part of the thighs and feet reaches 180 ° F and the juice becomes clear, pull the crispy chicken out of the grill.
5. Let the crispy grilled chicken rest under a loose foil tent for 15 minutes before eating.

72. Cajun Patch Cock Chicken

Prep Time: 30 minutes (additional 3 hours marinade); Cook Time: 2.5 hours

Servings: 4

INGREDIENTS:

➢ 4-5 pounds of fresh or thawed frozen chicken

➢ 4-6 glasses of extra virgin olive oil

➢ Cajun Spice Lab 4 tablespoons or Lucile Bloody Mary Mix Cajun Hot Dry Herb Mix Seasoning

DIRECTIONS:

1. Use hickory, pecan pellets, or blend to configure a wood pellet smoker grill for indirect cooking and preheat to 225 ° F.

2. If the unit has a temperature meat probe input, such as a MAK Grills 2 Star, insert the probe into the thickest part of the breast.

3. Make chicken for 1.5 hours.

4. After one and a half hours at 225 ° F, raise the pit temperature to 375 ° F and roast until the inside temperature of the thickest part of the chest reaches 170 ° F and the thighs are at least 180 ° F.

5. Place the chicken under a loose foil tent for 15 minutes before carving.

Roasted Tuscan Thighs

Prep Time: 20 minutes (plus 1-2 hours marinade); Cook Time: 40-60 minutes

Servings: 4

INGREDIENTS:

- ➢ 8 chicken thighs, with bone, with skin
- ➢ 3 extra virgin olive oils with roasted garlic flavor
- ➢ 3 cups of Tuscan or Tuscan seasoning per thigh

DIRECTIONS:

1. Set the wood pellet smoker grill for indirect cooking and use the pellets to preheat to 375 degrees Fahrenheit.

2. Depending on the grill of the wood pellet smoker, roast for 40-60 minutes until the internal temperature of the thick part of the chicken thigh reaches 180 ° F. Place the roasted Tuscan thighs under a loose foil tent for 15 minutes before serving.

Bone In-Turkey Breast

Prep Time: 20 minutes; Cook Time: 3-4 hours

Servings: 6-8

INGREDIENTS:

➢ 1 (8-10 pounds) boned turkey breast

➢ 6 tablespoons extra virgin olive oil

➢ 5 Yang original dry lab or poultry seasonings

DIRECTIONS:

1. Configure a wood pellet smoker grill for indirect cooking and preheat to 225 ° F using hickory or pecan pellets.

2. Smoke the boned turkey breast directly in a V rack or grill at 225 ° F for 2 hours.

3. After 2 hours of hickory smoke, raise the pit temperature to 325 ° F. Roast until the thickest part of the turkey breast reaches an internal temperature of 170 ° F and the juice is clear.

4. Place the hickory smoked turkey breast under a loose foil tent for 20 minutes, then scrape the grain.

Teriyaki Smoked Drumstick

Prep Time: 15 minutes (more marinade overnight); Cook Time: 1.5 hours to 2 hours

Servings: 4

INGREDIENTS:

- ➤ 3 cup teriyaki marinade and cooking sauce like Yoshida's original gourmet
- ➤ Poultry seasoning 3 tsp
- ➤ 1 tsp garlic powder
- ➤ 10 chicken drumsticks

DIRECTIONS:

1. Configure a wood pellet smoking grill for indirect cooking.
2. Place the skin on the drumstick and, while the grill is preheating, hang the drumstick on a poultry leg and wing rack to drain the cooking sheet on the counter. If you do not have a poultry leg and feather rack, you can dry the drumstick by tapping it with a paper towel.
3. Preheat wood pellet smoker grill to 180 ° F using hickory or maple pellets.
4. Make marinated chicken leg for 1 hour.

5. After 1 hour, raise the whole temperature to 350 ° F and cook the drumstick for another 30-45 minutes until the thickest part of the stick reaches an internal temperature of 180 ° F.

6. Place the chicken drumstick under the loose foil tent for 15 minutes before serving.

Hickory Spatchcock Turkey

Prep Time: 20 minutes; Cook Time: 3-4 hours

Servings: 8-10

INGREDIENTS:

➢ 1 (14 lb.) fresh or thawed frozen young turkey

➢ ¼ extra virgin olive oil with cup roasted garlic flavor

➢ 6 poultry seasonings or original dry lab in January

DIRECTIONS:

1. Configure a wood pellet smoking grill for indirect cooking and preheat to 225 ° F using hickory pellets.

2. Place the turkey skin down on a non-stick grill mat made of Teflon-coated fiberglass.

3. Suck the turkey at 225 ° F for 2 hours.

4. After 2 hours, raise the pit temperature to 350 ° F.

5. Roast turkey until the thickest part of the chest reaches an internal temperature of 170 ° F and the juice is clear.

6. Place the Hickory smoked roast turkey under a loose foil tent for 20 minutes before engraving.

Lemon Cornish Chicken Stuffed with Crab

Prep Time: 30 minutes (additional 2-3 hours marinade); Cook Time: 1 hour 30 minutes

Servings: 2-4

INGREDIENTS:

- ➢ 2 Cornish chickens (about 1¾ pound each)
- ➢ Half lemon, half
- ➢ 4 tbsp. western rub or poultry rub
- ➢ 2 cups stuffed with crab meat

DIRECTIONS:

1. Set wood pellet smoker grill for indirect cooking and preheat to 375 ° F with pellets.
2. Place the stuffed animal on the rack in the baking dish. If you do not have a rack that is small enough to fit, you can also place the chicken directly on the baking dish.
3. Roast the chicken at 375 ° F until the inside temperature of the thickest part of the chicken breast reaches 170 ° F, the thigh reaches 180 ° F, and the juice is clear.
4. Test the crab meat stuffing to see if the temperature has reached 165 ° F.

5. Place the roasted chicken under a loose foil tent for 15 minutes before serving.

Bacon Cordon Blue

Prep Time: 30 minutes; Cook Time: 2 to 2.5 hours

Servings: 6

INGREDIENTS:

- 24 bacon slices
- 3 large boneless, skinless chicken breasts, butterfly
- 3 extra virgin olive oils with roasted garlic flavor
- 3 Yang original dry lab or poultry seasonings
- 12 slice black forest ham
- 12-slice provolone cheese

DIRECTIONS:

1. Using apple or cherry pellets, configure a wood pellet smoker grill for indirect cooking and preheat (180 ° F to 200 ° F) for smoking.
2. Inhale bacon cordon blue for 1 hour.
3. After smoking for 1 hour, raise the pit temperature to 350 ° F.
4. Bacon cordon blue occurs when the internal temperature reaches 165 ° F and the bacon becomes crispy.
5. Rest for 15 minutes under a loose foil tent before serving.

Roast Duck à I Orange

Prep Time: 30 minutes; Cook Time: 2 to 2.5 hours; Servings: 3-4

INGREDIENTS:

➤ 1 (5-6 lb.) Frozen Long Island, Beijing, or Canadian ducks

➤ 3 tbsp. west or 3 tbsp.

➤ 1 large orange, cut into wedges

➤ Three celery stems chopped into large chunks

➤ Half a small red onion, a quarter

➤ Orange sauce:

➤ 2 orange cups

➤ 2 tablespoons soy sauce

➤ 2 tablespoons orange marmalade

➤ 2 tablespoons honey

➤ 3g tsp grated raw

DIRECTIONS:

1. Set the wood pellet smoker grill for indirect cooking and use the pellets to preheat to 350 ° F.

2. Roast the ducks at 350 ° F for 2 hours.

3. After 2 hours, brush the duck freely with orange sauce.

4. Roast the orange glass duck for another 30 minutes, making sure that the inside temperature of the thickest part of the leg reaches 165 ° F.

5. Place duck under loose foil tent for 20 minutes before serving.

6. Discard the orange wedge, celery, and onion. Serve with a quarter of duck with poultry scissors.

Herb Roasted Turkey

Prep Time: 30 minutes (additional 2-3 hours marinade); Cook Time: 1 hour 30 minutes

Servings: 2-4

INGREDIENTS:

- ➢ 8 Tbsp. Butter, Room Temperature
- ➢ 2 Tbsp. Mixed Herbs Such as Parsley, Sage, Rosemary, And Marjoram, Chopped
- ➢ 1/4 Tsp. Black Pepper, Freshly Ground
- ➢ 1 (12-14 Lbs.) Turkey, Thawed If pre-frozen.
- ➢ 3 Tbsp. Butter

DIRECTIONS:

1. In a small mixing bowl, combine the 8 tablespoons of softened butter, mixed herbs, and black pepper and beat until fluffy with a wooden spoon.
2. Remove any giblets from the turkey cavity and save them for gravy making, if desired. Wash the turkey, inside and out, under cold running water. Dry with paper towels.
3. Using your fingers or the handle of a wooden spoon, gently push some of the herbed butter underneath the turkey skin onto the breast halves, being careful not to tear the skin.

4. Rub the outside of the turkey with the melted butter and sprinkle with the Pit boss Pork and Poultry Rub. Pour the chicken broth in the bottom of the roasting pan.

5. When ready to cook, set temperature to 325 F and preheat, lid closed for 15 minutes.

Bourbon & Orange Brined Turkey

Prep Time: 30 minutes; Cook Time: 1 hour 30 minutes; Servings: 2-4

INGREDIENTS:

- Pit boss Orange Brine (From Kit)
- Pit boss Turkey Rub (From Kit)
- 1.25-2.5 Gallons Cold Water
- 1 Cup Bourbon
- 1 Tbsp. Butter, Melted

DIRECTIONS:

1. Mix Pit boss Orange Brine seasoning (from Orange Brine & Turkey Rub Kit) with one quart of water. Boil for 5 minutes. Remove from heat, add 1 gallon of cold water and bourbon.

2. Place turkey breast side down in a large container. Pour cooled brine mix over bird. Add cold water until bird is submerged. Refrigerate for 24 hours.

3. Remove turkey and disregard brine. Blot turkeys dry with paper towels. Combine butter and Grand Marnier and coat outside of turkey.

4. Season outside of turkey with Pit boss Turkey Rub (from Orange Brine & Turkey Rub Kit).

5. When ready to cook, set temperature to 225 F and preheat, lid closed for 15 minutes.

Pit boss Leftover Turkey Soup

Prep Time: 30 minutes; Cook Time: 1 hour 30 minutes; Servings: 2-4

INGREDIENTS:

- ➢ 1 Turkey Carcass
- ➢ 16 Cups Cold Water
- ➢ 2 Large Celery Ribs, Sliced
- ➢ 2 Large Carrots, Scraped and Sliced
- ➢ 2 Red Onions, Quartered

DIRECTIONS:

1. Strip a turkey carcass of all meat; set aside in a container.
2. Break up the bones of the turkey carcass and place them in a large pot. Add any turkey skin or other assorted "bits" that are not edible meat.
3. Once the stock has come to a boil, add all remaining Ingredients, and turn heat down until the bubbles barely break the surface. Let simmer for 3 to 4 hours, stirring occasionally.
4. When the stock is ready, strain it through a fine-meshed sieve into a large bowl; if your sieve is not fine, and line it first with cheesecloth.

5. Refrigerate stock, covered, for several hours or preferably overnight. You can either make soup the then day or freeze the stock.

Turkey by Rob's cooks

Prep Time: 30 minutes; Cook Time: 1 hour 30 minutes; **Servings:** 2-4

INGREDIENTS:

➢ Smoked Turkey by Rob's cooks

➢ 1 (12-14 Lb.) Turkey, Fresh or Thawed

➢ 3/4 Lb. (3 Sticks) Unsalted Butter

➢ 1 (5 Gal) Bucket or Stock Pot

➢ Foil Pan, Large Enough for Turkey

DIRECTIONS:

1. This method requires an overnight brining so collect everything the day before your meal.

2. The afternoon before, prepare your brine by adding the kosher salt and sugar to a medium saucepan. Cover with water and bring to a boil. Stir to dissolve the salt and sugar.

3. Prepare your turkey by removing the neck, gizzards, and truss, if pre-trussed. Trim off excess skin and fat near the cavity and neck. Place the turkey in bucket with the brine.

4. When ready to cook, set temperature to 180 F and preheat, lid closed for 15 minutes.

5. Remove your turkey from the brine. Remember there is a cavity full of water so make sure to do

this over the sink, otherwise you will have brine all over the place.

Traditional Thanksgiving Turkey

Prep Time: 30 minutes; Cook Time: 1 hour 30 minutes; Servings: 2-4

INGREDIENTS:

- ➢ 1 (18-20lb) Turkey
- ➢ 1/2 Lb. Butter, Softened
- ➢ 8 Sprigs Thyme
- ➢ 6 Cloves Garlic, Minced
- ➢ 1 Sprig Rosemary, Rough Chop

DIRECTIONS:

1. In a small bowl, combine butter with the minced garlic, thyme leaves, chopped rosemary, black pepper and kosher salt.
2. Prepare the turkey by separating the skin from the breast creating a pocket to stuff the butter-herb mixture in.
3. Cover the entire breast with 1/4" thickness of butter mixture.
4. Season the whole turkey with kosher salt and black pepper. As an option, you can also stuff the turkey cavity with Traditional Stuffing.
5. When ready to cook, set the temperature to 300 F and preheat, lid closed for 15 minutes.

Turkey Jalapeno Meatballs

Prep Time: 30 minutes; Cook Time: 1 hour 30 minutes; **Servings:** 2-4

INGREDIENTS:

- ➢ Turkey Jalapeño Meatballs
- ➢ 1 1/4 Lbs. Ground Turkey
- ➢ 1 Jalapeño Pepper, Deseeded and Finely Diced
- ➢ 1/2 Tsp Garlic Salt
- ➢ 1 Tsp Onion Powder

DIRECTIONS:

1. In a separate small bowl, combine the milk and breadcrumbs.
2. In a large bowl, mix turkey, garlic salt, onion powder, salt, pepper, Worcestershire sauce, cayenne pepper, egg, and jalapeños.
3. Add the bread crumb milk mixture to the bowl and combine. Cover with plastic and refrigerate for up to 1 hour.
4. When ready to cook, set the temperature to 350°F and preheat, lid closed for 15 minutes.
5. Roll the turkey mixture into balls, about one tablespoon each and place the meatballs in a single layer on a parchment lined baking sheet.

Wild Turkey Southwest Egg Rolls

Prep Time: 30 minutes; Cook Time: 1 **hour 30 minutes**; **Servings:** 2-4

INGREDIENTS:

➤ 2 Cups Leftover Wild Turkey Meat

➤ 1/2 Cup Corn

➤ 1/2 Cup Black Beans

➤ 3 Tbsp. Taco Seasoning

➤ 1/2 Cup White Onion, Chopped

DIRECTIONS:

1. Add olive oil to a large skillet and heat on the stove over medium heat. Add onions and peppers and sauté 2-3 minutes until soft. Add garlic, cook 30 seconds, then Rote and black beans.

2. Pour taco seasoning over meat and add 1/3 cup of water and mix to coat well. Add to veggie mixture and stir to mix well. If it seems dry, add 2 tbsp. water. Cook until heated all the way through.

3. Remove from the heat and transfer the mixture to the fridge. The mixture should be completely cooled prior to stuffing the egg rolls or the wrappers will break.

4. Place spoonful of the mixture in each wrapper and wrap tightly. Repeat with remaining wrappers.

When ready to cook, set temperature to High and preheat, lid closed for 15 minutes.

5. Brush each egg roll with oil or butter and place directly on the Pit boss grill grate. Cook until the exterior is crispy, about 20 min per side.

Nutrition: Calories 456, Total fat 37g, Saturated fat 13g, Total carbs 1g, Net carbs 1g Protein 124g, Sugars 0g, Fiber 0g, Sodium 1750mg

Grilled Wild Turkey Orange Cashew Salad

Prep Time: 30 minutes; Cook Time: 1 hour 30 minutes; Servings: 2-4

INGREDIENTS:

➢ Turkey Breast

➢ 2 Wild Turkey Breast Halves, Without Skin

➢ 1/4 Cup Teriyaki Sauce

➢ 1 Tsp Fresh Ginger

➢ 1 (12 Oz) Can Blood Orange Kill Cliff or Similar Citrus Soda

➢ 2 Tbsp. Pit boss Chicken Rub

➢ Cashew Salad

➢ 4 Cups Romaine Lettuce, Chopped

➢ 1/2 Head Red or White Cabbage, Chopped

➢ 1/2 Cup Shredded Carrots

➢ 1/2 Cup Edamame, Shelled

➢ 1 Smoked Yellow Bell Pepper, Sliced into Circles

➢ 1 Smoked Red Bell Pepper, Sliced into Circles

➢ 3 Chive Tips, Chopped

➢ 1/2 Cup Smoked Cashews

➢ Blood Orange Vinaigrette

➢ 1 Tsp Orange Zest

➢ Juice From 1/2 Large Orange

➢ 1 Tsp Finely Grated Fresh Ginger

> 2 Tbsp. Seasoned Rice Vinegar
> 1 Tsp Honey
> Sea Salt, To Taste
> 1/4 Cup Light Vegetable Oil

DIRECTIONS:

1. For the Marinade: Combine teriyaki sauce, Kill Cliff soda and fresh ginger. Pour marinade over turkey breasts in a Ziplock bag or dish and seal.

2. When ready to cook, set temperature to 375 F and preheat, lid closed for 15 minutes.

3. Remove turkey from the refrigerator, drain the marinade and pat turkey dry with paper towels.

4. Place turkey into a shallow oven proof dish and season with Pit boss Chicken Rub.

5. Place dish in the Pit boss and cook for 30-45 minutes or until the breast reaches an internal temperature of 160 F.

6. Remove the breast from the grill and wrap in Pit boss Butcher Paper. Let turkey rest for 10 minutes. While turkey is resting, prepare salad.

7. Assemble salad ingredients in a bowl and toss to mix. Combine all ingredients in list for vinaigrette.

8. After resting for 10 minutes, slice turkey and serve with cashew salad and blood orange vinaigrette. Enjoy!

Nutrition: Calories 956, Total fat 47g, Saturated fat 13g, Total carbs 1g, Net carbs 1g Protein 124g, Sugars 0g, Fiber 0g, Sodium 1750mg

Baked Cornbread Turkey Tamale Pie

Prep Time: 30 minutes; Cook Time: 1 hour 30 minutes; Servings: 2-4

INGREDIENTS:

Filling

- ➢ 2 Cups Shredded Turkey
- ➢ 2 Cobs of Corn
- ➢ 1 (15 Oz) Can Black Beans, Rinsed and Drained
- ➢ 1 Yellow Bell Pepper
- ➢ 1 Orange Bell Pepper
- ➢ 2 Jalapeños
- ➢ 2 Tbsp. Cilantro
- ➢ 1 Bunch Green Onions
- ➢ 1/2 Tsp Cumin
- ➢ 1/2 Tsp Paprika
- ➢ 1 (7 Oz) Can Chipotle Sauce
- ➢ 1 (15 Oz) Can Enchilada Sauce
- ➢ 1/2 Cup Shredded Cheddar Cheese

Cornbread Topping

- ➢ 1 Cup All-Purpose Flour
- ➢ 1 Cup Yellow or White Cornmeal
- ➢ 1 Tbsp. Sugar
- ➢ 2 Tsp Baking Powder
- ➢ 1/2 Tsp Salt

➢ 3 Tbsp. Butter

➢ 1 Cup Buttermilk

➢ 1 Large Egg, Lightly Beaten

DIRECTIONS:

1. For the filling: Mix to combine filling ingredients Place in the bottom of a butter greased 10-inch pan.

2. For the cornbread topping: In a mixing bowl, combine the flour, cornmeal, sugar, baking powder, and salt. Melt the butter in a small saucepan.

3. Add the milk-egg mixture to the dry ingredients and stir to combine. Do not over mix.

4. To assemble Tamale Pie: Fill the bottom of a butter greased 10-inch pan with the shredded turkey filling. Top with the cornbread topping and smooth to the edges of pan.

5. When ready to cook, set the temperature to 375 F and preheat, lid closed for 15 minutes.

6. Place directly on the grill grate and cook for 45-50 minutes or until the cornbread is lightly browned and cooked through. Enjoy!

Nutrition: Calories 956, Total fat 47g, Saturated fat 13g, Total carbs 1g, Net carbs 1g Protein 124g, Sugars 0g, Fiber 0g, Sodium 1750mg

Pit boss BBQ simple Turkey Sandwiches

Prep Time: 30 minutes; Cook Time: 45 minutes

Servings: 10

INGREDIENTS:

- ➢ 6 Turkey Thighs, Skin-On
- ➢ 1 1/2 Cups Chicken or Turkey Broth
- ➢ Pork & Poultry Rub
- ➢ 1 Cup barbeque Sauce, Or More as Needed
- ➢ 6 Buns or Kaiser Rolls, Split and Buttered

DIRECTIONS:

1. Season turkey thighs on both sides with the Pork & Poultry rub.
2. When ready to cook, turn temperature to 180 degrees F and preheat, lid closed for 15 minutes.
3. Arrange the turkey thighs exactly on the grill grate and smoke for 30 minutes.
4. Transfer the thighs to sturdy disposable aluminum foil or baking tray. Pour the broth around the thighs and then cover the pan with foil or a lid.
5. Increase temperature to 325 degrees F and preheat, lid closed. Roast the thighs until it reaches an internal temperature of 180 degrees F.

6. Remove pan from the grill but leave the grill on. Let the turkey thighs cool slightly up to they can be handled comfortably.

7. Let the drops drip off and keep. Remove skin and discard.

8. Pull out the shredded turkey meat with your fingers and return it to the roasting pan.

9. Add a cup or more of your favorite BBQ Sauce along with some of the drippings.

10. Recover the pan with foil and reheat the BBQ turkey on the grill for 20 to 30 minutes.

11. Serve with toasted buns if desired. Enjoy!

Nutrition: Energy (calories): 25 kcal; Protein: 0.7 g; Fat: 1.53 g ;Carbohydrates: 2.59 g

Roasted Spatchcock Turkey

Prep Time: 30 minutes

Cook Time: 3-4 hours

Servings: 4

INGREDIENTS:

- 1 (18-20 Lb.) Whole Turkey
- 4 tbsps. Turkey Rub
- 1 tbsp. Jacobsen Sea Salt
- 4 Cloves Garlic, Minced
- 3 tbsps. Parsley, Chopped.
- 1 tbsp. Rosemary, Chopped.
- 2 tbsps. Thyme Leaves, Chopped
- 2 Scallions, Chopped.
- 3 tbsps. Olive Oil

DIRECTIONS:

1. When ready to cook, turn temperature to High and preheat, lid closed for 15 minutes.

2. On a cutting board, mix the garlic, parsley, thyme, rosemary, and green onions. Chop the mixture until it turns into a paste. Set aside.

3. Spatchcock the turkey: With a large knife or shears, cut the bird open along the backbone on both sides, through the ribs, and remove the backbone.

4. Once the bird is open, split the breastbone to spread the bird flat, allowing it to roast evenly.

5. With the bird's breast facing up, season the outside with half of the Turkey Rub, then follow 2/3 of the herb mixture by rubbing it into the bird. Drizzle with olive oil.

6. Roll over the bird and then season generously with the remaining Turkey Rub.

7. Place the turkey exactly on the grill grate and cook for 30 minutes.

8. Turn to low temperature on the grill to 300 degrees F and continue to cook for 3-4 hours or until the internal temperature reaches 160 degrees F in the breast.

9. The finished inside temperature should reach 165 degrees F, but it will continue to rise after the bird is totally removed it from the grill.

10.   Prepare the bird and let it rest 20-25 minutes before carving. Enjoy!

Spatchcocked Maple Brined Turkey

Prep Time: 40 minutes; Cook Time: 2-3 hours

Servings: 6

INGREDIENTS:

- ➢ 1 (12-14 Lbs.) Turkey, Thawed If Frozen
- ➢ 5 Qtrs. Hot Water
- ➢ 1 1/2 Cups Kosher Salt
- ➢ 3/4 cup of Bourbon
- ➢ 1 cup of Pure Maple Syrup
- ➢ 1/2 Cup of Brown Sugar
- ➢ 1 Onion
- ➢ 3-4 Strips Orange Peel
- ➢ 3 Bay Leaves, Broken into Pieces
- ➢ 2 tbsps. Black Peppercorns
- ➢ 1 tbsp. Whole Cloves
- ➢ 3 Qtrs. Ice
- ➢ 1 cup Butter, Melted.
- ➢ Pork & Poultry Rub, As Needed
- ➢ Sprigs of Fresh Sage and Thyme, To Garnish
- ➢ Orange Wedges, Lady Apples, Or Kumquats, To Serve

DIRECTIONS:

For the Brine:

1. In a large stockpot or container, combine the hot water, kosher salt, bourbon, 3/4 cup of the maple syrup, brown sugar, onion, bay leaves, orange peel, peppercorns, and cloves and stir until well mixed. Add the ice.

2. Rinse or drain the turkey, inside and out, under cold running water. Remove giblets and discard or save for another use. Some turkeys come with a gravy packet as well; remove it before roasting the bird.

3. Add the turkey to the brine and refrigerate 8 to 12 hours, or overnight—weight with an ice pack to keep the bird immerse.

4. Rinse and pat dry it with paper towels; discard the brine.

5. Spatchcock the turkey: Using a knife or shears, cut the bird open along the spine on both sides, then through the ribs and removes the backbone.

6. Once the bird is open, split the breastbone to spread the bird flat, allowing it to roast evenly.

7. Mix the melted butter and the remaining 1/4 cup of maple syrup and divide in half. Brush half of the

blend on the bird and then sprinkle with Pork and Poultry Rub or the salt and black pepper.

8. Set aside the other half of the blend mixture until ready to use.

9. Prepare and ready to cook, set the temperature to 350 degrees F and preheat, lid closed for 15 minutes.

10. Roast or cook the turkey until the internal temperature in the thickest part of the breast reaches 165 degrees F, about 2-3 hours.

11. Brush with the remaining butter-maple syrup glaze while having the last 30 minutes of cooking the meat.

12. Let the turkey remain rest for 15 to 20 minutes and then garnish, if desired, with fresh herbs and or kumquats. Enjoy!

Home Turkey Gravy

Prep Time: 30 minutes; Cook Time: 3-4 hours

Servings: 8

INGREDIENTS:

- ➢ 4 cups Homemade Chicken Stock
- ➢ 2 Large Onions Cut Into 8th
- ➢ 4 Carrots, Rough Chop
- ➢ 4 Celery Stalks
- ➢ 8 Sprigs Thyme
- ➢ 8 Cloves Garlic, Peeled and Smashed
- ➢ 1 Turkey Neck
- ➢ 1 cup Flour
- ➢ 1 Stick Butter, Cut into About 8 Pieces
- ➢ 1 tsp. Kosher Salt
- ➢ 1 tsp. Cracked Black Pepper

DIRECTIONS:

1. When all are prepared ready to cook, set the temperature to 350 degrees and preheat with the lid closed for 15 minutes.

2. In a large pan, place turkey neck, plus onion, celery, also carrot, garlic, and thyme. Please add 4 cups of chicken stock and then sprinkle with salt and pepper.

49

3. Put the prepped turkey on the rack into the roasting pan and place it in the wood pellet grill.

4. Cook for 3-4 hours or until the breast reaches 160 degrees F. When you remove from the grill, the turkey will continue to cook and reach a finished internal temperature of 165degrees F.

5. Rinse the drippings into a saucepan and simmer on low.

6. In a larger saucepan, combine butter and flour with a whisk stirring until golden tan. It takes about 8 minutes, stirring constantly.

7. Next, whisk the drippings into the roux and cook until it comes to a boil. Season with salt and pepper and serve hot. Enjoy!

Roasted Honey Bourbon Glazed Turkey

Prep Time: 40 minutes; Cook Time: 3-4 hours

Servings: 8

INGREDIENTS:

- ➤ 1 (16-18 Lbs.) Turkey
- ➤ 1/4 Cup of Fin and Feather Rub
- ➤ Whiskey Glaze
- ➤ 1/2 cup Bourbon
- ➤ 1/2 Cup Honey
- ➤ 1/4 Cup Brown Sugar
- ➤ 3 tbsps. Apple Cider Vinegar
- ➤ 1 tbsp. Dijon Mustard
- ➤ Salt and Pepper, To Taste

DIRECTIONS:

1. Prepare and ready to cook, set the temperature to 375 degrees F and preheat, lid closed for 15 minutes.
2. Truss the turkey legs together and then season the exterior of the bird and the cavity with Fin and Feather Rub.
3. Place the turkey exactly on the grill grate and cook for 20-30 minutes at 375 degrees F or until the skin begins to brown.

4. After 30 minutes, turn down the temperature to 325 degrees F and continue to cook until the inside temperature registers 165 degrees F when an instant-read thermometer is inserted into the thickest part of the breast, about 3-4 hours.

For the Whiskey Glaze:

1. Blend or mix all ingredients in a small saucepan and bring to a boil. Turn down the heat and simmer for 15-20 minutes or until thick enough to cover the back of a spoon. Remove from heat and set aside.

2. Meanwhile the last ten minutes of cooking, brush the turkey's glaze while on the grill and cook until it is set, 10 minutes.

3. Remove from grill and let it rest 10-15 minutes before carving. Enjoy!

Roasted Autumn Brined Turkey Breast

Prep Time: 40 minutes; Cook Time: 3-4 hours

Servings: 6

INGREDIENTS:

- ➢ 6 Cups Apple Cider
- ➢ 2 Cloves Garlic, Smashed
- ➢ 1/3 Cup Brown Sugar
- ➢ 1 tbsp. Allspice
- ➢ 1/3 cup Kosher Salt
- ➢ 3 Bay Leaves
- ➢ 4 Cups Ice Water
- ➢ 1 Turkey Breast
- ➢ 1/2 Cup Plus Two Tbsps. Unsalted Butter, Softened
- ➢ Pork and Poultry Rub

DIRECTIONS:

For the Brine:

1. In a large pot or saucepan, Mix 4 cups of apple cider, the garlic cloves, brown sugar, allspice, salt, and bay leaves. Simmer on the stovetop for 5 minutes, stirring often.
2. Take off the stovetop and add in the ice water.

3. Put turkey in the brine and add water as needed until the turkey is fully submerged. Cover and refrigerate overnight.

For the Cider Glaze:

1. Let the remaining 2 cups of apple cider in a saucepan until reduced to 1/4 cup, about 30-45 minutes. Whisk in butter and cool completely.

2. After the turkey has brined overnight, drain the turkey and rinse.

3. Using your fingers, take two tablespoons of the softened butter and smear it under the breast's skin. Season the breast of the turkey with Pork & Poultry Rub.

4. When ready to cook, turn the temperature to 325 degrees F and preheat, lid closed for 15 minutes.

5. Cook turkey until it reaches an inside temperature of 160 degrees F, about 3-4 hrs. After the first 20 minutes of cooking, rub turkey with the cider glaze.

6. When the breast starts to get too dark you should cover it with foil. Let stand 30 minutes before carving. Enjoy!

BBQ Chicken Breasts

Prep Time: 40 minutes; Cook Time: 15 minutes

Servings: 6

INGREDIENTS:

- ➤ 4-6 Boneless and skinless Chicken Breast
- ➤ 1 half Cup of Sweet & Heat BBQ Sauce
- ➤ Salt and Pepper
- ➤ 1 tbsp. Chopped Parsley, To Garnish

DIRECTIONS:

1. Put the chicken breasts and a cup of Sweet & Heat BBQ sauce in a Ziploc bag and marinate overnight.

2. Turn temperature to High and preheat, lid closed for 15 minutes.

3. Remove chicken from marinade and season with salt and pepper.

4. Place directly on the grill grate and cook for 10 minutes on each side, flipping once or until the internal temperature reaches 150 degrees F.

5. Brush remaining sauce on chicken while on the grill and continue to cook 5-10 minutes longer or until a finished internal temperature of 165 degrees F.

6. Move away from grill and let rest 5 minutes before serving. Sprinkle with chopped parsley. Enjoy!

Wild Turkey Egg Rolls

Prep Time: 10 minutes; Cook Time: 55 minutes

Servings: 1

INGREDIENTS:

- Corn - ½ cup
- Leftover wild turkey meat - 2 cups
- Black beans - ½ cup
- Taco seasoning - 3 tablespoon
- Water ½ cup
- Rote chilies and tomatoes - 1 can
- Egg roll wrappers- 12
- Cloves of minced garlic- 4
- 1 chopped Poblano pepper or 2 jalapeno peppers
- Chopped white onion - ½ cup.

DIRECTIONS:

1. Add some olive oil to a large skillet. Heat it over medium heat on a stove.
2. Add peppers and onions. Sauté the mixture for 2-3 minutes until it turns soft.
3. Add some garlic and sauté for another 30 seconds. Add the Rote chilies and beans to the mixture. Keeping mixing the content gently. Reduce the heat and then simmer.

4. After about 4-5 minutes, pour in the taco seasoning and 1/3 cup of water over the meat. Mix everything and coat the meat well. If you feel that it is a bit dry, you can add 2 tablespoons of water. Keep cooking until everything is heated all the way through.

5. Remove the content from the heat and box it to store in a refrigerator. Before you stuff the mixture into the egg wrappers, it should be completely cool to avoid breaking the rolls.

6. Place a spoonful of the cooked mixture in each wrapper and then wrap it securely and tightly. Do the same with all the wrappers.

7. Preheat the Pit boss grill and brush it with some oil. Cook the egg rolls for 15 minutes on both sides, until the exterior is nice and crispy.

8. Remove them from the grill and enjoy with your favorite salsa!

BBQ Pulled Turkey Sandwiches

Prep Time: 30 minutes; Cook Time: 4 Hours

Servings: 1

INGREDIENTS:

➤ 6 skin-on turkey thighs

➤ 6 split and buttered buns

➤ 1 ½ cups of chicken broth

➤ 1 cup of BBQ sauce

➤ Poultry rub

DIRECTIONS:

1. Season the turkey thighs on both the sides with poultry rub.

2. Set the grill to preheat by pushing the temperature to 180 degrees F.

3. Arrange the turkey thighs on the grate of the grill and smoke it for 30 minutes.

4. Now transfer the thighs to an aluminum foil which is disposable and then pour the brine right around the thighs.

5. Cover it with a lid.

6. Now increase the grill, temperature to 325 degrees F and roast the thigh till the internal temperature reaches 180 degrees F.

7. Remove the foil from the grill but do not turn off the grill.

8. Let the turkey thighs cool down a little

9. Now pour the dripping and serve.

10. Remove the skin and discard it.

11. Pull the meat into shreds and return it to the foil.

12. Add 1 more cup of BBQ sauce and some more dripping.

13. Now cover the foil with lid and re-heat the turkey on the smoker for half an hour

14. Serve and enjoy.

Tempting Tarragon Turkey Breasts

Prep Time: 20 Minutes (Marinating Time: Overnight); Cook Time: 3½ to 4 hours

Servings: 4 to 5

INGREDIENTS:

For the marinade

- ¾ cup heavy (whipping) cream
- ¼ cup Dijon mustard
- ¼ cup dry white wine
- 2 tablespoons olive oil
- ½ cup chopped scallions, both white and green parts, divided.
- 3 tablespoons fresh tarragon finely chopped.
- 6 garlic cloves coarsely chopped.
    - 1 teaspoon salt
- 1 teaspoon freshly ground black pepper.

For the turkey:

- (6- to 7-pound) bone-in turkey breast
- ¼ cup (½ stick) unsalted butter, melted.

DIRECTIONS:

1. To make the marinade
2. In a large bowl, whisk together the cream, mustard, wine, and olive oil until blended.

3. Stir in ¼ cup of scallions and the tarragon, garlic, salt, and pepper.

4. Rub the marinade all over the turkey breast and under the skin. Cover and refrigerate overnight.

5. To make the turkey

6. Following the manufacturer's specific start-up procedure, preheat the smoker to 250°F, and add apple or mesquite wood.

7. Remove the turkey from the refrigerator and place it directly on the smoker rack. Do not rinse it.

8. Smoke the turkey for 3½ to 4 hours (about 30 minutes per pound), basting it with the butter twice during smoking, until the skin is browned and the internal temperature registers 165°F.

9. Remove the turkey from the heat and let it rest for 10 minutes.

10. Sprinkle with the remaining scallions before serving.

Juicy Beer Can Turkey

Prep Time: 20 Minutes; Cook Time: 6 hours

Servings: 6-8

INGREDIENTS:

For the rub

➢ 4 garlic cloves, minced.

➢ 2 teaspoons dry ground mustard

➢ 2 teaspoons smoked paprika.

➢ 2 teaspoons salt

➢ 2 teaspoons freshly ground black pepper.

➢ 1 teaspoon ground cumin

➢ 1 teaspoon ground turmeric

➢ 1 teaspoon onion powder

➢ ½ teaspoon sugar

For the turkey

➢ (10-pound) fresh whole turkey, neck, giblets, and gizzard removed and discarded.

➢ tablespoons olive oil

➢ 1 large, wide (24-ounce) can of beer, such as Foster's

➢ 4 dried bay leaves

➢ 2 teaspoons ground sage

➢ 2 teaspoons dried thyme

➢ ¼ cup (½ stick) unsalted butter, melted.

DIRECTIONS:

1. To make the rub
2. Following the manufacturer's specific start-up procedure, preheat the smoker to 250°F, and add cherry, peach, or apricot wood.
3. In a small bowl, stir together the garlic, mustard, paprika, salt, pepper, cumin, turmeric, onion powder, and sugar.
4. To make the turkey
5. Rub the turkey inside and out with the olive oil.
6. Apply the spice rub all over the turkey.
7. Pour out or drink 12 ounces of the beer.
8. Using a can opener, remove the entire top of the beer can.
9. Add the bay leaves, sage, and thyme to the beer.
10. Place the can of beer upright on the smoker grate. Carefully fit the turkey over it until the entire can is inside the cavity and the bird stands by itself. Prop the legs forward to aid in stability.
11. Smoke the turkey for 6 hours, basting with the butter every other hour.

12.   Remove the turkey from the heat when the skin is browned and the internal temperature registers 165°F. Remove the beer can very carefully—it will be slippery, and the liquid inside extremely hot. Discard the liquid and recycle the can.

13.   Let the turkey rest for 20 minutes before carving.

Buttered Thanksgiving Turkey

Prep Time: 25 minutes; Cook Time: 5 or 6 hours

Servings: 12 to 14

INGREDIENTS:

➢ 1 whole turkey (make sure the turkey is not pre-brined)

➢ 2 batches Garlic Butter Injectable

➢ 3 tablespoons olive oil

➢ 1 batch Chicken Rub

➢ 2 tablespoons butter

DIRECTIONS:

1. Supply your smoker with Traeger's and follow the manufacturer's specific start-up procedure. Preheat the grill, with the lid closed to 180°F.

2. Inject the turkey throughout with the garlic butter injectable. Coat the turkey with olive oil and season it with the rub. Using your hands, work the rub into the meat and skin.

3. Place the turkey directly on the grill grate and smoke for 3 or 4 hours (for an 8- to 12-pound turkey, cook for 3 hours; for a turkey over 12 pounds, cook for 4 hours), basting it with butter every hour.

4. Increase the grill's temperature to 375°F and continue to cook until the turkey's internal temperature reaches 170°F.

5. Remove the turkey from the grill and let it rest for 10 minutes, before carving and serving.

Jalapeno Injection Turkey

Prep Time: 15 minutes; Cook Time: 4 hours and 10 minutes;Servings: 6

INGREDIENTS:

- 15 pounds whole turkey, giblet removed.
- ½ of medium red onion, peeled and minced.
- 8 jalapeño peppers
- 2 tablespoons minced garlic
- 4 tablespoons garlic powder
- 6 tablespoons Italian seasoning
- 1 cup butter, softened, unsalted.

- ¼ cup olive oil
- 1 cup chicken broth

DIRECTIONS:

1. Open hopper of the smoker, add dry pallets, make sure ashcan is in place, then open the ash damper, power on the smoker, and close the ash damper.

2. Set the temperature of the smoker to 200 degrees F, let preheat for 30 minutes or until the green light on the dial blinks that indicate smoker has reached to set temperature.

3. Meanwhile, place a large saucepan over medium-high heat, add oil and butter and when the butter

melts, add onion, garlic, and peppers and cook for 3 to 5 minutes or until nicely golden brown.

4. Pour in broth, stir well, let the mixture boil for 5 minutes, then remove pan from the heat and strain the mixture to get just liquid.

5. Inject turkey generously with prepared liquid, then spray the outside of turkey with butter spray and season well with garlic and Italian seasoning.

6. Place turkey on the smoker grill, shut with lid, and smoke for 30 minutes, then increase the temperature to 325 degrees F and continue smoking the turkey for 3 hours or until the internal temperature of turkey reach to 165 degrees F.

7. When done, transfer turkey to a cutting board, let rest for 5 minutes, then carve into slices and serve.

Turkey Meatballs

Prep Time: 40 minutes; Cook Time: 40 minutes

Servings: 8

INGREDIENTS:

➢ 1 1/4 lb. ground turkey

➢ 1/2 cup breadcrumbs

➢ 1 egg, beaten.

➢ 1/4 cup milk

➢ 1 teaspoon onion powder

➢ 1/4 cup Worcestershire sauce

➢ Pinch garlic salt

➢ Salt and pepper to taste

➢ 1 cup cranberry jam

➢ 1/2 cup orange marmalade

➢ 1/2 cup chicken broth

DIRECTIONS:

1. In a large bowl, mix the ground turkey, breadcrumbs, egg, milk, onion powder, Worcestershire sauce, garlic salt, salt, and pepper.

2. Form meatballs from the mixture.

3. Preheat the Pit boss grill to 350 degrees F for 15 minutes while the lid is closed.

4. Add the turkey meatballs to a baking pan.

69

5. Place the baking pan on the grill.

6. Cook for 20 minutes.

7. In a pan over medium heat, simmer the rest of the ingredients for 10 minutes.

8. Add the grilled meatballs to the pan.

9. Coat with the mixture.

10.   Cook for 10 minutes.

Pit boss simple Smoked Turkey

Prep Time: 1 day and 1 hour; Cook Time: 4 hours and 30 minutes; Servings: 6

INGREDIENTS:

- 2 gallons of water, divided.
- 2 cups of sugar
- 2 cups salt
- Ice cubes
- 1 whole turkey
- ½ cup kosher salt
- ½ cup black pepper
- 3 sticks butter, sliced.

DIRECTIONS:

1. Add one-quart water to a pot over medium heat.
2. Stir in the 2 cups each of sugar and salt.
3. Bring to a boil.
4. Remove from heat and let cool.
5. Add ice and the remaining water.
6. Stir to cool.
7. Add the turkey to the brine.
8. Cover and refrigerate for 24 hours.
9. Rinse the turkey and dry with paper towels.
10. Season with salt and pepper.

11.   Preheat the Pit boss grill to 180 degrees F for 15 minutes while the lid is closed.

12.   Smoke the turkey for 2 hours.

13.   Increase temperature to 225 degrees. Smoke for another 1 hour.

14.   Increase temperature to 325 degrees. Smoke for 30 minutes.

15.   Place the turkey on top of a foil sheet.

16.   Add butter on top of the turkey.

17.   Cover the turkey with foil.

18.   Reduce temperature to 165 degrees F.

19.   Cook on the grill for 1 hour.

Maple Turkey Breast

Prep Time: 4 hours and 30 minutes; Cook Time: 2 hours; **Servings: 4**

INGREDIENTS:

- ➢ 3 tablespoons olive oil
- ➢ 3 tablespoons dark brown sugar
- ➢ 3 tablespoons garlic, minced.
- ➢ 2 tablespoons Cajun seasoning
- ➢ 2 tablespoons Worcestershire sauce
- ➢ 6 lb. turkey breast fillets

DIRECTIONS:

1. Combine olive oil, sugar, garlic, Cajun seasoning, and Worcestershire sauce in a bowl.
2. Soak the turkey breast fillets in the marinade.
3. Cover and marinate for 4 hours.
4. Grill the turkey at 180 degrees F for 2 hours.

Serving Suggestion: Let rest for 15 minutes before serving.

Preparation / Cooking Tips: You can also sprinkle dry rub on the turkey before grilling.

Nutrition:

Turkey with Apricot Barbecue Glaze

Prep Time: 30 minutes; Cook Time: 30 minutes

Servings: 4

INGREDIENTS:

- ➢ **4 turkey breast fillets**
- ➢ **4 tablespoons chicken rub**
- ➢ **1 cup apricot barbecue sauce**

DIRECTIONS:

1. Preheat the Pit boss grill to 365 degrees F for 15 minutes while the lid is closed.
2. Season the turkey fillets with the chicken run.
3. Grill the turkey fillets for 5 minutes per side.
4. Brush both sides with the barbecue sauce and grill for another 5 minutes per side.

Serving Suggestion: Serve with buttered cauliflower.

Preparation / Cooking Tips: You can sprinkle turkey with chili powder if you want your dish spicy.

Tandoori Chicken Wings

Prep Time: 20 minutes

Cook Time: 1 hour 20 minutes

Servings: 4-6

INGREDIENTS:

- ¼ Cup Yogurt
- 1 Whole Scallions, minced
- 1 Tablespoon minced cilantro leaves
- 2 Teaspoon ginger, minced.
- 1 Teaspoon Masala
- 1 Teaspoon salt
- 1 Teaspoon ground black pepper
- 1 ½ pound chicken wings
- ¼ cup yogurt
- 2 tablespoon mayonnaise
- 2 tablespoon Cucumber
- 2 teaspoon lemon juice
- ½ teaspoon cumin
- ½ teaspoon salt
- 1/8 cayenne pepper

DIRECTIONS:

1. Combine yogurt, scallion, ginger, garam masala, salt, cilantro, and pepper ingredients in the jar of a blender and process until smooth.

2. Put chicken and massage the bag to cat all the wings.

3. Refrigerate for 4 to 8 hours. Remove the excess marinade from the wings; discard the marinade.

4. Set the temperature to 350F and preheat, lid closed, for 10 to 15 minutes. Brush and oil the grill grate

5. Arrange the wings on the grill. Cook for 45 to 50 minutes, or until the skin is brown and crisp and meat is no longer pink at the bone. Turn once or twice during cooking to prevent the wings from sticking to the grill.

6. Meanwhile combine all sauce ingredients; set aside and refrigerate until ready to serve.

7. When wings are cooked through, transfer to a plate or platter. Serve with yogurt sauce.

Asian BBQ Chicken

Prep Time: 12 to 24 hours; Cook Time: 1 hour

Servings: 4-6

INGREDIENTS:

- ➢ 1 whole chicken
- ➢ To taste Asian BBQ Rub
- ➢ 1 whole ginger ale

DIRECTIONS:

1. Rinse chicken in cold water and pat dry with paper towels.

2. Cover the chicken all over with Asian BBQ rub; make sure to drop some in the inside too. Place in large bag or bowl and cover and refrigerate for 12 to 24 hours.

3. When ready to cook, set the Pit boss grill to 372F and preheat lid closed for 15 minutes.

4. Open can of ginger ale and take a few big gulps. Set the can of soda on a stable surface. Take the chicken out of the fridge and place the bird over top of the soda can. The base of the can and the two legs of the chicken should form a sort of tripod to hold the chicken upright.

5. Stand the chicken in the center of your hot grate and cook the chicken till the skin is golden brown

and the internal temperature is about 165F on an instant-read thermometer, approximately 40 minutes to 1 hour.

Homemade Turkey Gravy

Prep Time: 20 minutes; Cook Time: 3 hours 20 minutes; Servings: 8-12

INGREDIENTS:

- ➢ 1 turkey, neck
- ➢ 2 large Onion, eight
- ➢ 4 celeries, stalks
- ➢ 4 large carrots, fresh
- ➢ 8 clove garlic, smashed.
- ➢ 8 thyme sprigs
- ➢ 4 cup chicken broth
- ➢ 1 teaspoon chicken broth
- ➢ 1 teaspoon salt
- ➢ 1 teaspoon cracked black pepper.
- ➢ 1 butter, sticks
- ➢ 1 cup all-purpose flour

DIRECTIONS:

1. When ready to cook, set the temperature to 350F and preheat the Pit boss grill with the lid closed, for 15 minutes.

2. Place turkey neck, celery, carrot (roughly chopped), garlic, onion, and thyme on a roasting pan. Add four cups of chicken stock then season with salt and pepper.

3. Move the prepped turkey on the rack into the roasting pan and place in the Pit boss grill.

4. Cook for about 3-4 hours until the breast reaches 160F. The turkey will continue to cook, and it will reach a finished internal temperature of 165F.

5. Strain the drippings into a saucepan and simmer on low.

6. In a saucepan, mix butter (cut into 8 pieces) and flour with a whisk stirring until golden tan. This takes about 8 minutes, stirrings constantly.

7. Whisk the drippings into the roux then cook until it comes to a boil. Season with salt and pepper.

Bacon Wrapped Turkey Legs

Prep Time: 10 minutes; Cook Time: 3 hours

Servings: 4-6

INGREDIENTS:

➤ Gallon water

➤ To taste Pit boss rub

➤ ½ cup pink curing salt

➤ ½ cup brown sugar

➤ 6 whole peppercorns

➤ 2 whole dried bay leaves

➤ ½ gallon ice water

➤ 8 whole turkey legs

➤ 16 sliced bacon

DIRECTIONS:

1. In a large stockpot, mix one gallon of water, the rub, curing salt, brown sugar, peppercorns, and bay leaves.

2. Boil it to over high heat to dissolve the salt and sugar granules. Take off the heat then add in ½ gallon of ice and water.

3. The brine must be at least to room temperature, if not colder.

4. Place the turkey legs, completely submerged in the brine.

5. After 24 hours, drain the turkey legs then remove the brine.

6. Wash the brine off the legs with cold water, then dry thoroughly with paper towels.

7. When ready to cook, start the Pit boss grill according to grill instructions. Set the heat to 250F and preheat, lid closed for 10 to 15 minutes.

8. Place turkey legs directly on the grill grate.

9. After 2 ½ hours, wrap a piece of bacon around each leg then finish cooking them for 30 to 40 minutes of smoking.

10. The total smoking time for the legs will be 3 hours or until the internal temperature reaches 165F on an instant-read meat thermometer. Serve, Enjoy!

Roasted Chicken

Prep Time: 20 minutes; Cook Time: 1 hour 20 minutes; **Servings:** 4-6

INGREDIENTS:

➢ 8 tablespoon butter, room temperature

➢ 1 clove garlic, minced.

➢ 1 scallion, minced.

➢ 2 tablespoon fresh herbs such as thyme, rosemary, sage, or parsley

➢ As needed Chicken rub

➢ Lemon juice

➢ As needed vegetable oil

DIRECTIONS:

1. In a small cooking bowl, mix the scallions, garlic, butter, minced fresh herbs, 1-1/2 teaspoon of the rub, and lemon juice. Mix with a spoon.

2. Remove any giblets from the cavity of the chicken. Wash the chicken inside and out with cold running water. Dry thoroughly with paper towels.

3. Sprinkle a generous amount of Chicken Rub inside the cavity of the chicken.

4. Gently loosen the skin around the chicken breast and slide in a few tablespoons of the herb butter under the skin and cover.

5. Cover the outside with the remaining herb butter.

6. Insert the chicken wings behind the back. Tie both legs together with a butcher's string.

Powder the outside of the chicken with more Chicken Rub then insert sprigs of fresh herbs inside the cavity of the chicken.

7. Set temperature to High and preheat, lid closed for 15 minutes.

8. Oil the grill with vegetable oil. Move the chicken on the grill grate, breast-side up then close the lid.

9. After chicken has cooked for 1 hour, lift the lid. If chicken is browning too quickly, cover the breast and legs with aluminum foil.

10. Close the lid then continue to roast the chicken until an instant-read meat thermometer inserted into the thickest part registers a temperature of 165F.

11. Take off chicken from grill and let rest for 5 minutes. Serve, Enjoy!

Grilled Asian Chicken Burgers

Prep Time: 5 minutes; Cook Time: 50 minutes

Servings: 4-6

INGREDIENTS:

- ➢ Pound chicken, ground
- ➢ 1 cup panko breadcrumbs
- ➢ 1 cup parmesan cheese
- ➢ 1 small jalapeno, diced.
- ➢ 2 whole scallions, minced.
- ➢ 2 garlic cloves
- ➢ ¼ cup minced cilantro leaves
- ➢ 2 tablespoon mayonnaise
- ➢ 2 tablespoon chili sauce
- ➢ 1 tablespoon soy sauce
- ➢ 1 tablespoon ginger, minced.
- ➢ 2 teaspoon lemon juice
- ➢ 2 teaspoon lemon zest
- ➢ 1 teaspoon salt
- ➢ 1 teaspoon ground black pepper
- ➢ 8 hamburger buns
- ➢ 1 tomato, sliced.
- ➢ Arugula, fresh
- ➢ 1 red onion sliced.

DIRECTIONS:

1. Align a rimmed baking sheet with aluminum foil then spray with nonstick cooking spray.

2. In a large bowl, combine the chicken, jalapeno, scallion, garlic, cilantro, panko, Parmesan, chili sauce, soy sauce ginger, mayonnaise, lemon juice and zest, and salt and pepper.

3. Work the mixture with your fingers until the ingredients are well combined. If the mixture looks too wet to form patties and add additional more panko.

4. Wash your hands under cold running water, form the meat into 8 patties, each about an inch larger than the buns and about ¾" thick. Use your thumbs or a tablespoon, make a wide, shallow depression in the top of each.

5. Put them on the prepared baking sheet. Spray the tops with nonstick cooking spray. If not cooking right away, cover with plastic wrap and refrigerate.

6. Set the Pit boss grill to 350F then preheat for 15 minutes, lid closed.

7. Order the burgers, depression-side down, on the grill grate. Remove and discard the foil on the

baking sheet so you will have an uncontaminated surface to transfer the slider when cooked.

8. Grill the burgers for about 25 to 30 minutes, turning once, or until they release easily from the grill grate when a clean metal spatula is slipped under them. The internal temperature when read on an instant-read meat thermometer should be 160F.

9. Spread mayonnaise and arrange a tomato slice, if desired, and a few arugulas leaves on one-half of each bun. Top with a grilled burger and red onions, if using, then replace the top half of the bun. Serve immediately. Enjoy

Grilled Sweet Cajun Wings

Prep Time: 10 minutes; Cook Time: 45 minutes

Servings: 4-6

INGREDIENTS:

➢ 2-pound chicken wings

➢ As needed Pork and Poultry rub

➢ Cajun shake

DIRECTIONS:

1. Coat wings in Sweet rub and Cajun shake.

2. When ready to cook, set the Pit boss grill to 350F and preheat, lid closed for 15 minutes.

3. Cook for 30 minutes until skin is brown and center is juicy, and an instant-read thermometer reads at least 165F. Serve, Enjoy!

The Grilled Chicken Challenge

Prep Time: 15 minutes ;Cook Time: 1 hour and 10 minutes; Servings: 4-6

INGREDIENTS:

➤ 1 (4-lbs.) whole chicken

➤ As needed chicken rub

DIRECTIONS:

1. When ready to cook, set temperature to 375F then preheat, close the lid for 15 minutes.

2. Rinse and dry the whole chicken (remove and discard giblets, if any). Season the entire chicken, including the inside of the chicken using chicken rub.

3. Place the chicken on the grill and cook for 1 hour and 10 minutes.

4. Remove chicken from grill when internal temperature of breast reaches 160F. Check heat periodically throughout as cook times will vary based on the weight of the chicken.

5. Allow chicken to rest until the internal temperature of breast reaches 165F, 15-20 minutes. Enjoy!

114. Chicken Breast with Lemon

Prep Time: 15min;Cook Time: 15min

Servings: 6

INGREDIENTS:

➢ 6 Chicken breasts, skinless and boneless

➢ ½ cup Oil

➢ 1 - 2 Fresh thyme sprigs

➢ 1 tsp. ground black pepper

➢ 2 tsp. Salt

➢ 2 tsp. of Honey

➢ 1 Garlic clove, chopped.

➢ 1 Lemon the juice and zest

➢ For service: Lemon wedges

DIRECTIONS:

1. In a bowl combine the thyme, black pepper, salt, honey, garlic, and lemon zest and juice. Stir until dissolved and combined. Add the oil and whisk to combine.

2. Clean the breasts and pat dry. Place them in a plastic bag. Pour the pre-made marinade and massage to distribute evenly. Place in the fridge, 4 hours.

3. Preheat the grill to 400F with the lid closed.

4. Drain the chicken and grill until the internal temperature reaches 165F, about 15 minutes.

5. Serve with lemon wedges and a side dish of your choice.

Nutrition:

Chicken Breasts with Dried Herbs

Prep Time: 15 minutes; Cook Time: 40 minutes

Servings: 4

INGREDIENTS:

- ➢ 4 chicken breasts boneless
- ➢ 1/4 cup garlic-infused olive oil
- ➢ 2 clove garlic minced.
- ➢ 1/4 tsp of dried sage
- ➢ 1/4 tsp of dried lavender
- ➢ 1/4 tsp of dried thyme
- ➢ 1/4 tsp of dried mint
- ➢ 1/2 Tbsps. dried crushed red pepper
- ➢ Kosher salt to taste

DIRECTIONS:

1. Place the chicken breasts in a shallow plastic container.
2. In a bowl, combine all remaining ingredients, and pour the mixture over the chicken breast and refrigerate for one hour.
3. Remove the chicken breast from the sauce (reserve sauce) and pat dry on kitchen paper.
4. Start your Pit boss grill on SMOKE (hickory Traeger) with the lid open until the fire is established). Set

the temperature to 250F and preheat for 10 to 15 minutes.

5. Place chicken breasts on the smoker. Close Pit boss grill lid and cook for about 30 to 40 minutes or until chicken breasts reach 165F.

6. Serve hot with reserved marinade.

Grilled Chicken with Pineapple

Prep Time: 1 hour Cook Time: 1 hr. 15; Servings: 6

INGREDIENTS:

➢ 2 lbs. Chicken tenders

➢ 1 c. sweet chili sauce

➢ ¼ c. fresh pineapple juice

➢ ¼ c. honey

DIRECTIONS:

1. Combine the honey, pineapple juice, and sweet chili sauce in a medium bowl. Whisk together thoroughly.

2. Put ¼ cup of the mixture to one side.

3. Coat the chicken in the sauce.

4. Place a lid over the bowl and leave it in the fridge for 30 minutes to marinate.

5. Heat the grill to high heat.

6. Separate the chicken from the marinade and grill for 5 minutes on each side.

7. Use the reserved sauce to brush over the chicken.

8. Continue to grill for a further 1 minute on each side.

9. Take the chicken off the grill and let it rest for 5 minutes before servings.

Whole Orange Chicken

Prep Time: 15 minutes + marinate time.

Cook Time: 45 minutes; Servings: 4

INGREDIENTS:

- ➢ 1 whole chicken, 3-4 pounds' backbone removed.
- ➢ 2 oranges
- ➢ ¼ cup oil
- ➢ 2 teaspoons Dijon mustard
- ➢ 1 orange, zest
- ➢ 2 tablespoons rosemary leaves, chopped.
- ➢ 2 teaspoons salt

DIRECTIONS:

1. Clean and pat your chicken dry.
2. Take a bowl and mix in orange juice, oil, orange zest, salt, rosemary leaves, Dijon mustard and mix well.
3. Marinade chicken for 2 hours or overnight
4. Pre-heat your grill to 350 degrees F
5. Transfer your chicken to the smoker and smoke for 30 minutes' skin down. Flip and smoke until the internal temperature reaches 175 degrees F in the thigh and 165 degrees F in the breast.
6. Rest for 10 minutes and carve.
7. Enjoy!

Turkey Patties

Prep Time: 20 minutes; Cook Time: 40 minutes

Servings: 6

INGREDIENTS:

➢ 2 lbs. turkey minced meat

➢ 1/2 cup of parsley finely chopped.

➢ 2/3 cup of onion finely chopped.

➢ 1 red bell pepper finely chopped.

➢ 1 large egg at room temperature

➢ Salt and pepper to taste

➢ 1/2 tsp dry oregano

➢ 1/2 tsp dry thyme

DIRECTIONS:

1. In a bowl, combine well all ingredients.

2. Make from the mixture patties.

3. Start Pit boss grill on (recommended apple or oak Traeger) lid open, until the fire is established (4-5 minutes). Increase the temperature to 350F and allow to pre-heat, lid closed, for 10 - 15 minutes.

4. Place patties on the grill racks and cook with lid covered for 30 to 40 minutes.

5. Your turkey patties are ready when you reach a temperature of 130F.

6. Serve hot.

Special Occasion's Dinner Cornish Hen

Prep Time: 15 minutes; Cook Time: 1 hour

Servings: 4

INGREDIENTS:

- ➢ 4 Cornish game hens
- ➢ 4 fresh rosemary sprigs
- ➢ 4 tbsp. butter, melted.
- ➢ 4 tsp. chicken rub

DIRECTIONS:

1. Set the temperature of Grill to 375 degrees F and preheat with closed lid for 15 mins.
2. With paper towels, pat dry the hens.
3. Tuck the wings behind the backs and with kitchen strings, tie the legs together.
4. Coat the outside of each hen with melted butter and sprinkle with rub evenly.
5. Stuff each hen with a rosemary sprig.
6. Place the hens onto the grill and cook for about 50-60 mins.
7. Remove the hens from grill and place onto a platter for about 10 mins.
8. Cut each hen into desired-sized pieces and serve.

Crispy & Juicy Chicken

Prep Time: 15 minutes; Cook Time: 5 hours

Servings: 6

INGREDIENTS:

- ¾ C. dark brown sugar
- ½ C. ground espresso beans
- 1 tbsp. ground cumin
- 1 tbsp. ground cinnamon
- 1 tbsp. garlic powder
- 1 tbsp. cayenne pepper
- Salt and ground black pepper, to taste
- 1 (4-lb.) whole chicken, neck and giblets removed.

DIRECTIONS:

1. Set the temperature of Grill to 200-225 degrees F and preheat with closed lid for 15 mins.
2. In a bowl, mix brown sugar, ground espresso, spices, salt, and black pepper.
3. Rub the chicken with spice mixture generously.
4. Put the chicken onto the grill and cook for about 3-5 hours.
5. Remove chicken from grill and place onto a cutting board for about 10 mins before carving.
6. Cut the chicken into desired-sized pieces and serve.

Ultimate Tasty Chicken

Prep Time: 15 minutes; Cook Time: 3 hours

Servings: 5

INGREDIENTS:

For Brine:

➢ 1 C. brown sugar

➢ ½ C. kosher salt

➢ 16 C. water

For Chicken:

➢ 1 (3-lb.) whole chicken

➢ 1 tbsp. garlic, crushed.

➢ 1 tsp. onion powder

➢ Salt

➢ Ground black pepper, to taste

➢ 1 medium yellow onion, quartered.

➢ 3 whole garlic cloves, peeled.

➢ 1 lemon, quartered.

➢ 4-5 fresh thyme sprigs

DIRECTIONS:

1. For brine: in a bucket, dissolve brown sugar and kosher salt in water.

2. Place the chicken in brine and refrigerate overnight.

3. Set the temperature of Grill to 225 degrees F and preheat with closed lid for 15 mins.

4. Remove the chicken from brine and with paper towels, pat it dry.

5. In a small bowl, mix crushed garlic, onion powder, salt, and black pepper.

6. Rub the chicken with garlic mixture evenly.

7. Stuff the inside of the chicken with onion, garlic cloves, lemon, and thyme.

8. With kitchen strings, tie the legs together.

9. Place the chicken onto grill and cook, covered for about 2½-3 hours.

10. Remove chicken from pallet grill and transfer onto a cutting board for about 10 mins before carving.

11. Cut the chicken in desired sized pieces and serve.

Ultimate Tasty Chicken

Prep Time: 15 minutes; Cook Time: 3 hours

Servings: 5

INGREDIENTS:

For Brine:

- ➢ 1 C. brown sugar
- ➢ ½ C. kosher salt
- ➢ 16 C. water

For Chicken:

- ➢ 1 (3-lb.) whole chicken
- ➢ 1 tbsp. garlic, crushed.
- ➢ 1 tsp. onion powder
- ➢ Salt
- ➢ Ground black pepper, to taste
- ➢ 1 medium yellow onion, quartered.
- ➢ 3 whole garlic cloves, peeled.
- ➢ 1 lemon, quartered.
- ➢ 4-5 fresh thyme sprigs

DIRECTIONS:

1. For brine: in a bucket, dissolve brown sugar and kosher salt in water.

2. **Place the chicken in brine and refrigerate overnight.**

3. Set the temperature of Grill to 225 degrees F and preheat with closed lid for 15 mins.

4. Remove the chicken from brine and with paper towels, pat it dry.

5. *In a small bowl, mix crushed garlic, onion powder, salt, and black pepper.*

6. Rub the chicken with garlic mixture evenly.

7. Stuff the inside of the chicken with onion, garlic cloves, lemon, and thyme.

8. With kitchen strings, tie the legs together.

9. Place the chicken onto grill and cook, covered for about 2½-3 hours.

10. Remove chicken from pallet grill and transfer onto a cutting board for about 10 mins before carving.

11. Cut the chicken in desired sized pieces and serve.

South-East-Asian Chicken Drumsticks

Prep Time: 15 minutes;Cook Time: 2 hours

Servings: 6

INGREDIENTS:

- ➢ 1 C. fresh orange juice
- ➢ ¼ C. honey
- ➢ 2 tbsp. sweet chili sauce
- ➢ 2 tbsp. hoisin sauce
- ➢ 2 tbsp. fresh ginger grated finely.
- ➢ 2 tbsp. garlic, minced.
- ➢ 1 tsp. Sriracha
- ➢ ½ tsp. sesame oil
- ➢ 6 chicken drumsticks

DIRECTIONS:

1. Set the temperature of Grill to 225 degrees F and preheat with closed lid for 15 mins, using charcoal.
2. Mix all the ingredients except for chicken drumsticks and mix until well combined.
3. Set aside half of honey mixture in a small bowl.
4. In the bowl of remaining sauce, add drumsticks and mix well.
5. Arrange the chicken drumsticks onto the grill and cook for about 2 hours, basting with remaining sauce occasionally.

Game Day Chicken Drumsticks

Prep Time: **15 minutes; Cook Time**: **1 hour**

Servings: 8

INGREDIENTS:

For Brine:

- ½ C. brown sugar
- ½ C. kosher salt
- 5 C. water
- 2 (12-oz.) bottles beer
- 8 chicken drumsticks
- For Coating:
- ¼ C. olive oil
- ½ C. BBQ rub
- 1 tbsp. fresh parsley, minced.
- 1 tbsp. fresh chives, minced.
- ¾ C. BBQ sauce
- ¼ C. beer

DIRECTIONS:

1. For brine: in a bucket, dissolve brown sugar and kosher salt in water and beer.
2. Place the chicken drumsticks in brine and refrigerate, covered for about 3 hours.

3. Set the temperature of Grill to 275 degrees F and preheat with closed lid for 15 mins.

4. Remove chicken drumsticks from brine and rinse under cold running water.

5. *With paper towels, pat dry chicken drumsticks.*

6. Coat drumsticks with olive oil and rub with BBQ rub evenly.

7. Sprinkle the drumsticks with parsley and chives.

8. Arrange the chicken drumsticks onto the grill and cook for about 45 mins.

9. Meanwhile, in a bowl, mix BBQ sauce and beer.

10. Remove from grill and coat the drumsticks with BBQ sauce evenly.

11. Cook for about 15 mins more.

12. Serve immediately.

Glazed Chicken Thighs

Prep Time: 15 minutes;Cook Time: 2 hours and 5 minutes; Servings: 4

INGREDIENTS:

➢ 2 garlic cloves, minced.

➢ ¼ C. honey

➢ 2 tbsp. soy sauce

➢ ¼ tsp. red pepper flakes, crushed.

➢ 4 (5-oz.) skinless, boneless chicken thighs

➢ 2 tbsp. olive oil

➢ 2 tsp. sweet rub

➢ ¼ tsp. red chili powder

➢ Freshly ground black pepper, to taste

DIRECTIONS:

1. Set the temperature of Grill to 400 degrees F and preheat with closed lid for 15 mins.

2. In a bowl, add garlic, honey, soy sauce and red pepper flakes and with a wire whisk, beat until well combined.

3. Coat chicken thighs with oil and season with sweet rub, chili powder and black pepper generously.

4. Arrange the chicken drumsticks onto the grill and cook for about 15 mins per side.

5. In the last 4-5 mins of cooking, coat the thighs with garlic mixture.
6. Serve immediately.

CPSIA information can be obtained
at www.ICGtesting.com
Printed in the USA
BVHW042008250621
610384BV00010B/385